BEST CANADIAN POLITICAL CARTOONS 1984

JOHN LARTER
The Toronto Star, October 13, 1983

BEST CANADIAN POLITICAL CARTOONS 1984

edited by
N.M. Stahl

foreword by
Robert La Palme

McClelland and Stewart

ISBN: 0-7710-5873-X

McClelland and Stewart Limited
The Canadian Publishers
25 Hollinger Road
Toronto, Ontario M4B 3G2

First printing September, 1984

Produced by:

Miller Services Limited
45 Charles Street East
Toronto, Ontario M4Y 1S6
Stock photo library and newspaper feature syndicate

Design and typesetting by Five Seven Nine Design, Toronto

Printed and bound in Canada

Front cover: Blaine, *The Hamilton Spectator*, June 1984
Back cover: Dennis Pritchard, freelance, Shallow Lake (Ont.), April 6, 1984

Foreword

Going through the *Guinness Book of World Records*, one is amazed to notice that it is always possible for man to surpass his achievements. Yesterday, Jerry Turnbull ran the mile in four minutes, thirty-five seconds, today Paul Ankel beats him by two seconds, tomorrow Bugs Bunny will do it in half a second! The longest reign at the Canadian prime minister's office was Mackenzie King's — a record Pierre chose not to challenge — so he filled the padding of the PM's chair with razor blades before passing it over to his dear friend John Turner, who, traumatized, has since developed a buttock complex and is actually establishing a fanny-slapping record.

Man continues to outdo himself. Confederation's first half-century saw the emergence of outstanding cartoonists. The most celebrated were Bengough, Brunet, Bourgeois, and Racey. Then we went through a period of self-conscious artists development to reach, at last, today's superb editorial cartooning.

Bengough   Brunet   Bourgeois   Racey

It is difficult to believe that today's quality will be surpassed in the future. You can see what I mean if you leaf through this book.

Robert La Palme o.c., RCA
Director: International Salon of Cartoons

Table of Contents

Introduction

Joey Smallwood, former premier of Newfoundland, once remarked that political cartoons, friendly or unfriendly, are so good that he hated to see them wasted on his opponents.[1] Mr. Smallwood likely realized what political cartoonists are quick to argue — that they cause no more harm to politicians than the politicians cause to themselves. Indeed, cartoonists do not create controversy, they simply make their living on the controversy created by others.

Satire is the foremost function of political cartooning. Its end is always "the good": social reform, truth, fair play. Its means are scorn and ridicule, presented most often in a humorous manner. Political cartoonists today no longer have to "toe the line" for the newspaper editorials; instead, they are their own free agents and are responsible for their stand. Power and privilege of government are typical targets of the cartoonist's satire. But popular opinion can come under fire, too, as in the cartoon by Ting on page 168 which mocks Canadian opposition to the testing of the cruise missiles.

Humour is the most effective vehicle of the cartoonist's message. And why shouldn't we be entitled to some comic relief in the face of ever-disheartening news? How often do we get a chance to laugh at a deficit, or political patronage, or Revenue Canada? Humour, though, is not essential to the medium. Witness the cartoon by Aislin on page 157, which makes a sobering comment on war and on Canada's two solitudes.

Artistic merit, admittedly a contentious issue in any visual medium, weighs less heavily in political cartooning. This is not to say that the exquisite penmanship of such masters as Roy Peterson and Edd Uluschak should go unnoticed. Rather, it suggests that the message is more important than its appearance. For example, the relatively unsophisticated drawing style of Mike Constable hardly diminishes the force of his attack on acid rain in his cartoon on page 163.

Caricature, the exaggeration of distinctive physical features for comic effect, is widely employed by Canada's political cartoonists. It takes little time for them to seize on perceived peculiarities and expand them to comic, even grotesque, proportions. The caricature of Jean Chrétien by Jim Todd on page 32 pulls no punches in this respect.

Political cartoonists comprise a tiny elite in Canada. In this country of 25 million people, only some thirty-odd individuals earn a living from this form of cartooning. And until this year, when Sue Dewar joined *The Calgary Sun*, all have been male. Most of their work is virtually unknown outside the readership of their respective newspapers. This collection, in its second annual edition, is meant to share the best of these political cartoons for wider appreciation and enjoyment.

Nicholas M. Stahl
August 1984

1. *The Hecklers: two centuries of Canadian political cartooning.* National Film Board of Canada: 1975. Made by Ian McLaren. Conceived by Terry Mosher.

Acknowledgements

Once again it has been my privilege to have Robert La Palme on the editorial panel and, this year, as the author of the foreword. Following his retirement from a prolific cartooning career that spanned almost forty years, Mr. La Palme now devotes much of his time to the preservation and celebration of political cartoons. Each year in Montreal, he directs the world-renowned International Salon of Cartoons, which he founded in 1964. The vitality of this septuagenarian is simply inspirational.

I am also grateful for the participation of Nick Auf der Maur, who replaces David Rosen on the editorial panel this year. Mr. Auf der Maur, who recently co-authored a biography of Brian Mulroney, is well known to Montrealers. He has been a television producer and director, a city councillor, a *Gazette* columnist, and is currently contesting a seat in the federal election.

Most of the research required for the texts herein was carried out by my assistant, Eliane St-Louis. Her untiring effort has been much appreciated.

Thanks are also due to Jim Cherrier, manager of the Toronto Star Syndicate, and Bill Cassidy of Canada Wide Feature Services, both of whom generously assisted in preparing submissions for this book.

1983 National
Newspaper Award

Dale Cummings has been the staff editorial cartoonist of the *Winnipeg Free Press* since 1982. Born in St. Thomas, Ontario, he studied animation and illustration at Sheridan College in Oakville. Cummings sold his first political cartoon to *The London Free Press* in 1968 and since then has placed cartoons on a freelance basis in many periodicals, including *Canadian Forum, The Last Post, Maclean's, The Globe and Mail,* and the *New York Times.*

Winnipeg Free Press, January 19, 1983

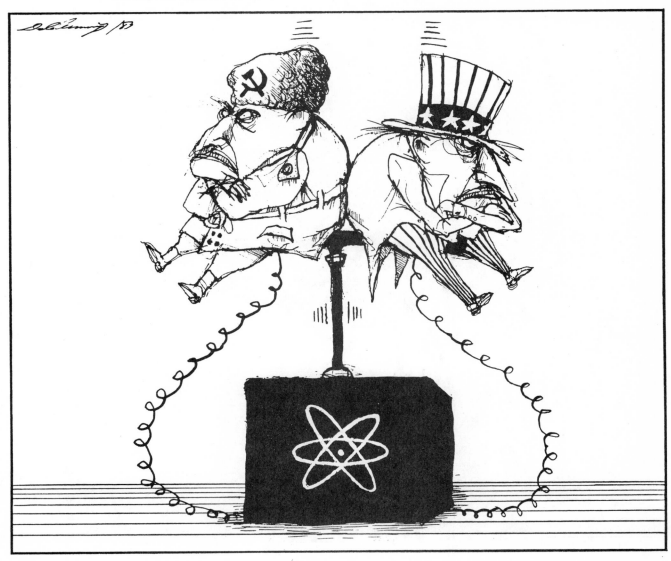

End of the Trudeau Era

After fifteen years as leader of the Liberal party, and as prime minister for almost as long, Pierre Trudeau faced mounting pressure to retire, even from within his party. In fact, almost eight out of ten respondents to a Southam News poll published on September 10 wanted Trudeau to resign. Only a day earlier, he had protested to a gathering of party faithful in Lac Delage, Quebec, that he was not a quitter.

MIKE ASHMORE
The Times, Oshawa (Ont.), July 30, 1983

ANDY DONATO
The Toronto Sun, September 13, 1983

ANDY DONATO
The Toronto Sun, December 11, 1983

Canadians had already been jaded by a false resignation call. After his long reign in power was interrupted briefly by Joe Clark in 1979, Pierre Trudeau announced his retirement and called for a leadership convention the following spring. But shortly after his party defeated the Progressive Conservatives in a non-confidence vote the same year, Trudeau revealed that he would stay on as Liberal leader for a last election campaign.

TING (Merle Tingley)
The London Free Press, February 2, 1983

On February 29, a date that can be commemorated only once every four years, Prime Minister Pierre Trudeau finally made his decisive announcement. Popular support for the Liberals was lagging about twenty points behind that for the Tories, and news of his resignation promptly spurred gains in the Canadian stock markets and in the value of the Canadian dollar.

"YOU'RE RIGHT, IT DOES LOOK LIKE MARGARET TRUDEAU'S HUSBAND!"

TING (Merle Tingley)
The London Free Press, December 15, 1983

VANCE RODEWALT
The Calgary Herald, March 1, 1984

In her reply to Mr. Trudeau's letter of resignation, Iano Campagnolo, president of the Liberal party of Canada, wrote: "The many triumphs of your years as prime minister will soon become the inevitable stuff of history."

JOSH BEUTEL
The Telegraph-Journal, Saint John (N.B.), March 5, 1984

ADRIANE RAESIDE
The Times-Colonist, Victoria, March 6, 1984

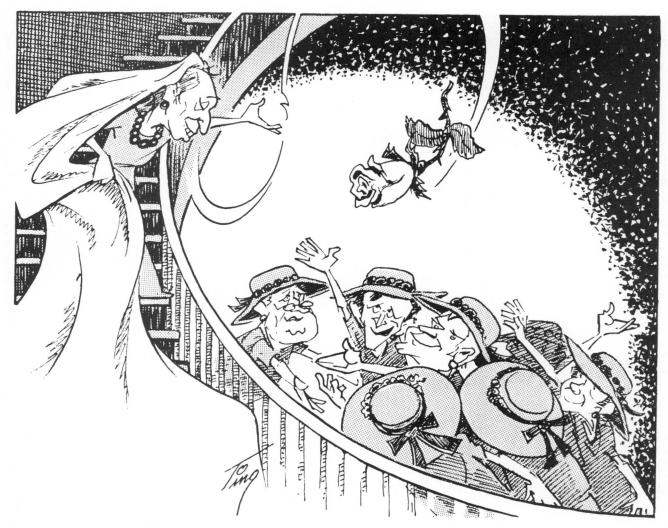

TING (Merle Tingley)
The London Free Press, June 14, 1984

On the eve of the Liberal party's leadership convention, the tribute to outgoing Prime Minister Trudeau was nostalgic and emotional. Answering speculation about his future endeavours, he replied in an interview, "What I want to do is precisely nothing, besides moving to Montreal, buying a car, getting the kids in school, hiring a maid, and that sort of thing."

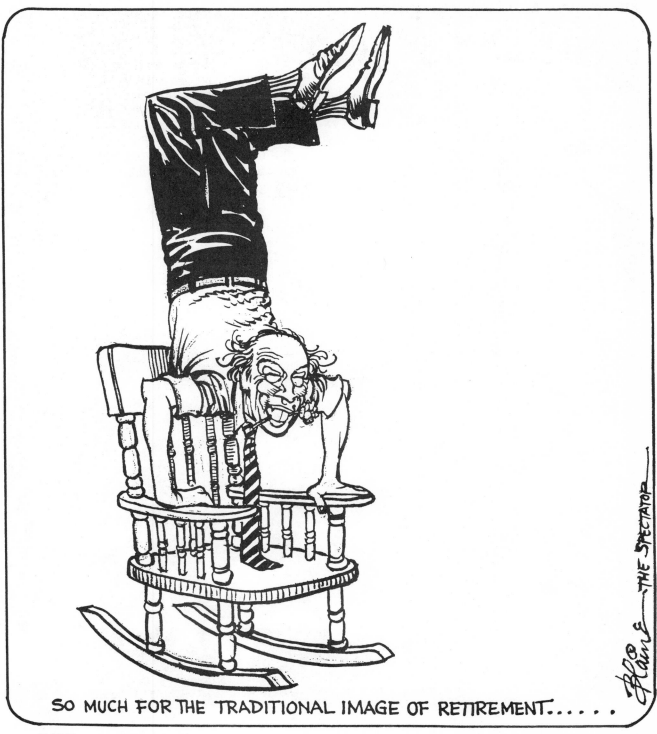

SO MUCH FOR THE TRADITIONAL IMAGE OF RETIREMENT......

BLAINE
The Hamilton Spectator, June 12, 1984

The Liberal Leadership Convention

Liberal cabinet ministers wasted little time considering whether to enter the leadership contest. Shortly after Prime Minister Trudeau's letter of resignation on February 29, six came forth: Donald Johnston (economic development), Mark MacGuigan (justice), John Roberts (employment), Jean Chrétien (energy), Eugene Whelan (agriculture), and John Munro (Indian affairs). However, most attention was tuned to former Finance Minister John Turner's decision to enter the fray. Even before his announcement on March 16, a string of cabinet ministers declared their support for Mr. Turner, giving him a lead from the outset.

SNOW WHITE AND THE SEVEN DWARFS.

TONY JENKINS
The Globe and Mail, Toronto, March 20, 1984

ALAN KING
The Citizen, Ottawa, March 17, 1984

JOHN LARTER
The Toronto Star, March 22, 1984

John Napier Turner, an accomplished corporate lawyer, first entered politics in 1962 and assumed several cabinet portfolios under Pearson and Trudeau administrations. But he resigned suddenly, and without reason, in 1975 while minister of finance, during a time when the government's spending and deficits were climbing tremendously. As Trudeau's popularity waned in recent years, Turner's grew, and he became, in the eyes of many people, the preferred leader of the Liberal party. Expectation that he would announce his candidacy was so great that the media played considerably on his indecision before March 16.

"You'll have to speak up, John."

EDD ULUSCHAK
The Edmonton Journal, March 8, 1984

LEN NORRIS
The Sun, Vancouver, March 17, 1984

"Isn't it exciting! The people who gave us Trudeaumania are about to give us Turnermania!"

John Turner soon was widely acknowledged as the front-running candidate. Bucking unfavourable attention to his departure from politics eight years ago, his "Bay Street" image, and the perception of him as a right-winger, Turner campaigned largely on several popular issues. He pledged to halve the deficit, to trim the size of the cabinet, to assist unemployed youth, to promote women's rights, to support small enterprise, and to continue efforts to further nuclear disarmament.

FRANK EDWARDS
The Whig-Standard, Kingston (Ont.), March 21, 1984

AISLIN (Terry Mosher)
The Gazette, Montreal, April 11, 1984

SUE DEWAR
The Calgary Sun, March 20, 1984

Promptly after announcing his candidacy, John Turner placed himself under much criticism for remarks he made about the contentious French-language-rights debate in Manitoba. He declared that the issue, which already had been addressed to the Supreme Court of Canada, was a provincial matter and that it ought to be resolved "by the political process and not by the judicial process." The remarks embarrassed his own party and drew support from Quebec's Parti Québécois minister Gerald Godin, since that party has long advocated provincial jurisdiction in the area of language legislation.

BADO (Guy Badeaux)
Le Droit, Ottawa, March 22, 1984

The perfect bilingual

MIKE GRASTON
The Windsor Star, March 27, 1984

DUNCAN MACPHERSON
The Toronto Star, March 21, 1984

Turner promptly qualified his remarks on Manitoba's language issue. To quell the embarrassing furore, he allowed that the federal government and the courts have a responsibility to intervene "at times" to protect fundamental rights, but he stopped short of declaring it a federal responsibility to extend French-language services in the provinces.

FRANK EDWARDS
The Whig-Standard, Kingston (Ont.), date unavailable

Energy Minister Jean Chrétien formally announced his candidacy on March 22, beginning what was to become a passionate campaign for his election as Liberal leader. From the start, he had to contend with the Liberal party's weighty tradition of alternating English- and French-language leaders: "A lot of people say that because I am a francophone I cannot be a candidate. I thought that we were all equal in Canada, but some say that I am less equal than others . . . I have to reflect on that."

JIM TODD
Cameron Publications, N.S., March 14, 1984

BOB KRIEGER
The Province, Vancouver, March 26, 1984

Nevertheless, Chrétien, of all the cabinet ministers, was given the best odds of winning the leadership race. It was speculated that he was the candidate favoured by Prime Minister Trudeau, with whom he had a long and close association in politics.

CORKY (Violette Clark)
New Westminster Now, B.C., May 1984

JUST YOU WATCH THE LITTLE GUY FROM SHAWINIGAN COME OUT OF THIS RACE WITH EXCELLENT GRADES!

JIM TODD
Cameron Publications, N.S., June 6, 1984

Right:

Right:

Eugene Whelan, minister of agriculture, ran a modest-sized campaign and distinguished himself by always wearing a large western hat at his appearances. The media seized on a remark he made that seemed quite prejudicial: "A man should always wear a hat. . . . In summer, the sun'll roast your brains if you don't wear a hat. That's one reason they have low IQs in Africa, they don't wear hats." The remark preceded a more serious comment on malnutrition and an announcement that he would be chairing the World Food Council's conference in Ethiopia.

ANTHONY DELATRI
Le Nouvelliste, Trois-Rivieres (Que.), June 2, 1984

Jean Chrétien as seen by the western separatists

MIKE GRASTON
The Windsor Star, June 2, 1984

AISLIN (Terry Mosher)
The Gazette, Montreal, April 21, 1984

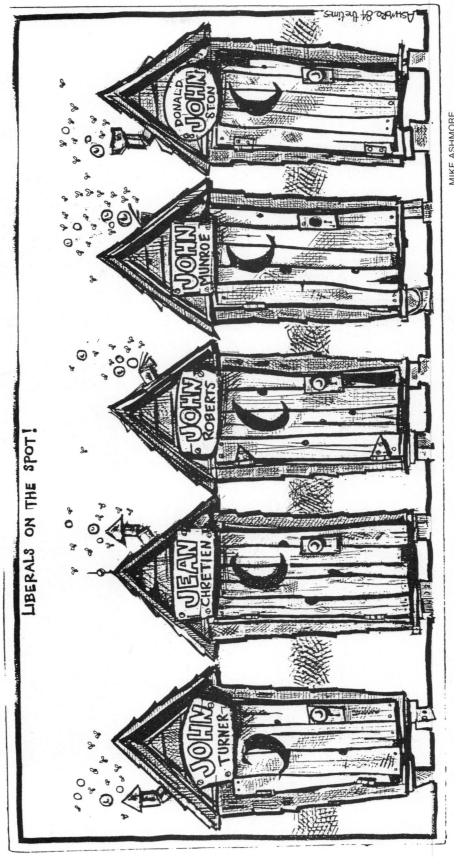

MIKE ASHMORE
The Times, Oshawa (Ont.), April 14, 1984

Public support for the Liberal party, as indicated by the Gallup poll, slipped after Prime Minister Trudeau announced his retirement. It fell to a mere 32 per cent of decided respondents, versus 54 per cent for the Progressive Conservatives, in a poll released on April 5. However, this situation changed dramatically the following month. By May 1, the Gallup poll indicated a remarkable recovery in support for the Liberals, to 46 per cent of decided respondents, versus 40 per cent for the Conservatives.

EDD ULUSCHAK
The Edmonton Journal, March 23, 1984

BLAINE
The Hamilton Spectator, June 14, 1984

ROY PETERSON
The Sun, Vancouver, June 8, 1984

"*Avoid messy second-ballot sag!*"

JIM TODD
Cameron Publications, N.S., June 16, 1984

John Turner was victorious. By the second ballot, he had beaten his six rivals by commanding 54.4 per cent of the votes. Second place Jean Chrétien, who collared 40 per cent of the final vote, was lauded affectionately by party president Iona Campagnolo as "the man who came in second, but first in our hearts." Regardless of which candidate was victorious, Trudeau promised at the outset of the convention, "You will see me there following him."

ADRIANE RAESIDE
The Times-Colonist, Victoria, June 17, 1984

ANDY DONATO
The Toronto Sun, June 17, 1984

To fulfil his pledge to rebuild the Liberal party, Prime Minister Designate John Turner was expected to pay particular attention to Liberal favour in the western provinces. He made one step towards realizing that commitment by announcing his intention to seek a seat in British Columbia during the election expected in 1984.

BOB BIERMAN
Freelance, Victoria, date unavailable

HAWTHORN GRODER: CHICKEN RANCHER

DALE CUMMINGS
Winnipeg Free Press, June 19, 1984

Negotiations were hectic as Prime Minister Designate John Turner hurriedly assembled a new cabinet for his administration. In a sweeping array of dismissals, appointments, reassignments, and amalgamations announced on June 30, he created a cabinet of twenty-nine members, eight fewer than Trudeau's. Jean Chrétien, Turner's closest rival in the leadership race, was expected to play an important role in the new cabinet, and he did. Turner promoted him to deputy prime minister, and minister of external affairs, the most senior portfolio. Chrétien would also become the party's Quebec lieutenant, considered to be an important role for the anglo-led government.

LEN NORRIS
The Sun, Vancouver, June 22, 1983

"If Mr. Turner does give a whole province to Mr. Chrétien, the least you should put in for is a decent-sized town . . . ."

FRANK EDWARDS
The Whig-Standard, Kingston (Ont.), June 22, 1984

DENNIS PRITCHARD
Freelance, Shallow Lake (Ont.), June 22, 1984

AISLIN (Terry Mosher)
The Gazette, Montreal, May 16, 1984

Towards the Federal Election

Public support for the Liberals and the Tories seesawed before the Liberal leadership convention. Neither party held a consistent and decisive margin over the other. The two leaders themselves, both of corporate backgrounds, were widely perceived as "look-alike" candidates who did not seriously pit themselves against each other on the issues. The contest, it seemed, was one of image. The only dramatic factor in the public's sentiment was the steadily falling support for the New Democratic Party. Support among decided voters fell to a twenty-four-year low of 11 per cent, according to Gallup polls.

EDD ULUSCHAK
The Edmonton Journal, June 20, 1984

"On your marks, get set . . ."

JOSH BEUTEL
The Telegraph-Journal, Saint John (N.B.), June 22, 1984

0 613012

0 613013

TONY JENKINS
The Globe and Mail, Toronto, June 19, 1984

THE REAL WINNER

BICKERSTAFF (Don Evans)
The Orillia Sun, (Ont.), June 20, 1984

The Federal Government

DENNIS PRITCHARD
Freelance, Shallow Lake (Ont.), November 4, 1983

A major victory was won by metrication opponents when, on November 1, the Ontario Provincial Court dismissed a crown suit against two gasoline station operators for selling their product by the gallon. In their defence, Judge William Ross cited the Charter of Rights and Freedoms and found the Weights and Measures Act unnecessarily severe and also negligent for not specifically prohibiting the Imperial measure. Some Tory MPs had also challenged the metric system law that year by operating a maverick gas station near Ottawa. However, their provocation went unchallenged.

Below:

A significant aspect of the Charter of Rights and Freedoms is that it undermines the doctrine of parliamentary supremacy — the unwritten convention inherited from Great Britain that gives Parliament virtually unlimited legislative power. A challenge by a coalition opposing the government's planned testing of U.S. cruise missiles was accepted by the federal court on the grounds that such testing might be argued to violate the new constitution's guarantees of life, liberty, and security of person. The judiciary therefore has the power to overrule Parliament and the government of Canada, if it deems constitutional rights and freedoms have been breached.

Right:

Earlier in 1983, the federally-owned aerospace firm, Canadair, reported a record Canadian corporate loss of $1.4 billion from the previous year. Drastic measures were announced in October to trim these losses. Ten of the company's twenty-two vice-presidential jobs would be eliminated and another 338 jobs cut by year's end.

DUNCAN MACPHERSON
The Toronto Star, October 15, 1983

JOHN LARTER
The Toronto Star, October 21, 1983

DUNCAN MACPHERSON
The Toronto Star, December 12, 1983

Left:
Commitment to worldwide peace and military disarmament were among policies central to Prime Minister Trudeau's government, as described in the Speech from the Throne, read by Governor General Edward Schreyer on December 7.

Below:
Jean-Claude Parrot, president of the 23,000-member Canadian Union of Postal Workers, made an unsuccessful attempt to protest the fact that Canada Post allowed companies to mail material at bulk letter rates as low as 13.5 cents while charging individuals 32 cents. Parrot announced that for one week in December mail sorters would accept greeting cards and letters with only 10 cents postage. The Canadian Labour Relations Board promptly ruled that the action would constitute an illegal strike and demanded that Parrot retract the plan.

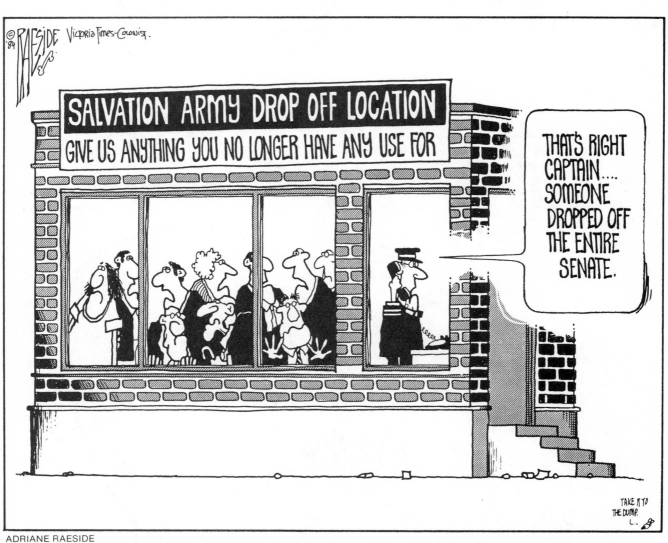

ADRIANE RAESIDE
The Times-Colonist, Victoria, February 3, 1984

The Senate, which is comprised of members appointed by the prime minister, performs a largely symbolic — some say ineffectual — role in government. The joint committee of Parliament, given the mandate of studying the issue of Senate reform, released a report on January 31 that recommended the Senate be an elected assembly. The report also advocated more representation for the smaller provinces and a stronger mandate for the Senate to check more effectively the powers of the Commons. The government made no immediate commitment to act on the proposals.

ANTHONY DELATRI
Le Nouvelliste, Trois-Rivières (Que.), February 11, 1984

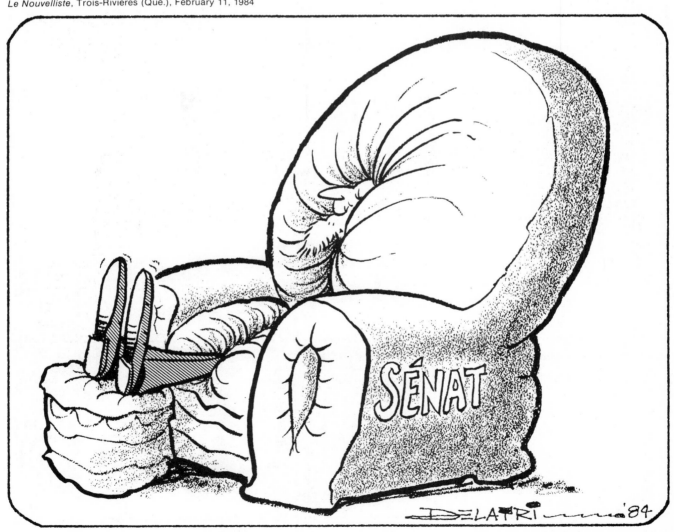

Below:

Prime Minister Trudeau rewarded five loyal Liberals and associates with appointments to the Senate on January 13, bringing to eight the number of appointments made since December 1983. Although thirteen vacancies still remained, Trudeau would make a total of eight more appointments before retiring on June 30. Diplomatic posts were also conferred on allies of the prime minister.

Right:

A second constitutional conference between the first ministers and native leaders March 8 and 9 failed to achieve consensus on an amendment guaranteeing the right of native people to self-government. Prime Minister Trudeau tabled a proposed amendment that would have guaranteed the principle, but not the details, of native self-government, but several premiers rejected the proposal. Two more such conferences are to be held by 1987.

JOSH BEUTEL
The Telegraph-Journal, Saint John (N.B.), January 26, 1984

...and so, we in Ottawa will continue to negotiate as long as the leaves grow on the trees, the rivers flow free, etc. Frankly, if this matter was resolved, thousands of civil servants here at Indian Affairs would then be thrown out of work.

AISLIN (Terry Mosher)
The Gazette, Montreal, March 22, 1984

A brief tempest erupted when it was alleged that funds from the Special Employment Initiatives Program were appropriated mainly for Liberal-held ridings. *Maclean's* magazine reported that Liberal MPs were given several months' advance notice to apply for job-creation and special-project funds while opposition MPs were notified later, when most of the funds had been appropriated. Employment Minister John Roberts, Finance Minister Marc Lalonde, and Prime Minister Trudeau all denied the accusation.

ROY PETERSON
The Sun, Vancouver, February 24, 1984

JOHN ROBERTS' WEATHER REPORT

COLD FRONT

WARM FRONT

"... heavy slush in Toronto with 76 per cent chance of windfalls in Liberal ridings across the country, as well as intermittent but perfectly natural dry spells in opposition constituencies ..."

Below:

An attempt by Finance Minister Marc Lalonde to embarrass opposition leader Brian Mulroney backfired, and prompted the minister to make an apology before the House. When confronted with a question about unemployed people, Lalonde thought he had a written representation by Mulroney made during his corporate career that sought "an advantage for the rich." When the letter in question was presented to the Commons, a red-faced Marc Lalonde found himself presenting evidence that suggested quite the opposite picture of Brian Mulroney.

Right:

After a lengthy parliamentary debate and the deliberations of a special Senate committee, legislation to create a civilian spy agency was re-introduced on January 18. The proposed Canadian Security Intelligence Service would assume responsibility for national security — currently in the hands of the RCMP — but would enjoy much broader powers.

ALAN KING
The Citizen, Ottawa, February 1, 1984

DALE CUMMINGS
Winnipeg Free Press, February 17, 1984

TONY JENKINS
The Globe and Mail, Toronto, February 7, 1984

Revenue Canada drew much criticism this year for the heavy-handed manner in which it audited some individuals for income tax assessment. The Progressive Conservatives quickly rose to the offence, accusing Revenue Canada of abusing taxpayers, and formed a task force to conduct public hearings across the country to expose further the government's practices. One practice particularly in question was the use of quotas in some localities to determine the amount of taxes auditors were expected to recover from undeclared taxable income.

SID BARRON
The Toronto Star, March 16, 1984

"... Peter, you know those fascinating little collages I've got ... you know, the ones you made by cutting up your income tax forms ... well, there's a Revenue Canada person here now and he's ... uh ..."

ROI (Roy Carless)
Canadian Transport, Ottawa, April 1984

Among the proposals resulting from the Tory task force were a curtailment of Revenue Canada's powers of search and seizure, and the abolishment of quotas on taxing undeclared income. Taxpayers, the Tories insisted, should be considered innocent in tax cases until proven otherwise.

BOB KRIEGER
The Province, Vancouver, February 5, 1984

MIKE GRASTON
The Windsor Star, May 11, 1984

Left:
The Grange Commission was formed to investigate the circumstances of thirty-six infant deaths at Toronto's Hospital for Sick Children in 1980 and 1981 that were caused by overdoses of the drug digoxin. One year later, the commission began to release the names of nurses it suspected had administered the overdoses. The Ontario Court of Appeal quickly ruled that such findings were not admissible because they tended to discriminate without offering the protection of a trial, and therefore violated a person's civil rights.

Below:
Prime Minister Trudeau was among the world leaders who, along with thousands of Second World War veterans, met on June 6 at Normandy, France, site of the historic D-Day invasion by Allied forces against the Nazis forty years ago.

Trudeau's Peace Mission

Prime Minister Trudeau, during the last months before he announced his retirement, embarked on an ambitious personal mission to promote worldwide peace and nuclear disarmament. In the first stage of his tour, he met leaders of Asian, Persian Gulf, and European nations. His trip later continued to the United States, where he met with President Reagan and other senior administrators. While Reagan generally supported Trudeau's peace initiative, the president stopped short of committing the United States to any of Trudeau's specific proposals, such as a summit conference of the five major nuclear powers. Reagan declared that he sought a military balance between East and West blocs, and Trudeau indicated that he was satisfied with the outcome of the talks.

ROY PETERSON
The Sun, Vancouver, December 16, 1983

"All I want, Santa, is peace on earth and good will to all men who haven't achieved nuclear superiority."

BADO (Guy Badeaux)
Le Droit, Ottawa, December 16, 1983

Trudeau-Reagan meeting: *"I met him halfway!"*

BICKERSTAFF (Don Evans)
The Orillia Sun (Ont.), November 23, 1983

PILGRIM'S PROGRESS

ROI (Roy Carless)
Canadian Transport, Ottawa, November 1983

"HE'S NOT USED TO FLYING!"

DALE CUMMINGS
Winnipeg Free Press, January 20, 1984

ADRIANE RAESIDE
The Times-Colonist, Victoria, January 31, 1984

A visit with Soviet leader Yuri Andropov was regarded as an important conclusion to the prime minister's peace mission. Trudeau had already won the support of the North Atlantic Treaty Organization for his plan, and in January he took his mission to several East European nations as a prelude to a hoped-for visit to Moscow. By now, many leaders of both East and West bloc nations praised Trudeau for his efforts to improve constructive dialogue between the camps.

FRANK EDWARDS
The Whig-Standard, Kingston (Ont.), February 11, 1984

Left:
The death of Yuri Andropov momentarily thwarted Prime Minister Trudeau's efforts to conclude his peace tour with a visit to Moscow.

Below:
New Democratic Party leader Ed Broadbent pointed to "the illogical folly" of Trudeau's peace proposals in light of his administration's decision to proceed with the testing of the cruise missile in Canada.

BOB BIERMAN
Freelance, Victoria, date unavailable

The Loyal Opposition

Under the watchful eye of television audiences, Brian Mulroney took his seat in the Commons for the first time on September 12, 1983. He had been leader of the Progressive Conservatives since June but had been confined to the press gallery until he handily won a by-election in Nova Scotia on August 29. Prime Minister Trudeau, who was visiting Greece at that time, said he welcomed Mulroney's election and would treat him with "respect and apprehension."

DALE CUMMINGS
Winnipeg Free Press, September 9, 1983

DUNCAN MACPHERSON
The Toronto Star, September 3, 1983

ANDY DONATO
The Toronto Sun, September 11, 1983

EDD ULUSCHAK
The Edmonton Journal, February 4, 1984

The emphasis appeared to be more on style than content as Brian Mulroney made his first appearances in Parliament as leader of the opposition. Although polls suggested that the Tories were enjoying extremely high levels of voter support at the time, Mulroney was quickly criticized for not being forthright on the issues.

GAMBOLI (Tony Harpes)
The Gazette, Montreal, September 16, 1983

MIKE GRASTON
The Windsor Star, September 14, 1983

JOHN LARTER
The Toronto Star, November 25, 1983

BLAINE
The Hamilton Spectator, February 1984

Brian Mulroney, his wife Mila, and their three children finally moved into Stornoway, the official Ottawa residence of the leader of the opposition. The elderly house had undergone $79,000 worth of renovations since Joe Clark and his family left.

YEARNING FOR ADOPTION

BLAINE
The Hamilton Spectator, December 5, 1983

The Progressive Conservatives continued to hold sway over the Liberals in general public support. But a Gallup poll released in January revealed that support for the Tories was much higher among men than among women: 60 per cent versus 46 per cent of decided respondents respectively.

JOHN LARTER
The Toronto Sun, January 10, 1984

JOHN LARTER
The Toronto Sun, May 3, 1984

GAMBOLI (Tony Harpes)
The Gazette, Montreal, March 24, 1984

Once the Liberal party's leadership race was in full tilt, with John Turner enjoying much of the media's attention, Tory fortunes fell almost overnight. Not even Turner's bumbling of the Manitoba language-rights issue was enough to tarnish seriously his credibility in the eyes of voters. On May 1, Gallup reported the greatest turnaround of popular support over one month ever observed in forty-two years. Favour for the Tories among decided respondents plummeted from 54 per cent in March to 40 per cent in April, while Liberal support soared from 32 per cent to 46 per cent over the same period.

ROY PETERSON
The Sun, Vancouver, June 21, 1984

Opposition leader Brian Mulroney was anxious to put his party back on the front page after the devastating effect that the publicity given to John Turner had on Tory fortunes. Mulroney met with U.S. President Ronald Reagan and senior administrators for two days, using the occasion to criticize former Prime Minister Trudeau's handling of relations between the two countries. Mulroney's position on a variety of issues did not differ substantially from Trudeau's, but the Tory leader sought to win Americans' support by assuring them that he would avoid a confrontational manner in dealing with the United States.

JOHN LARTER
The Toronto Star, June 19, 1984

The Economy

The prospects for continued economic recovery, following the recession of 1981-82, were uncertain. The rate of inflation from mid-1983 to mid-1984 remained stable and modest. The Gross National Product — the widest measure of economic growth — increased noticeably in 1983 after the decline of the previous year. But high interest rates, in keeping with American levels, appeared to be aggravating economic growth and unemployment. A secret cabinet report, which was ostensibly prepared by Economic Development Minister Donald Johnston and which found its way into the hands of opposition MPs, contained harsh criticism for certain federal departments, including finance. Prompted by the report, Tory MP John Crosbie questioned Prime Minister Trudeau: "Is it correct that the departments are run so badly that Canada now lacks some of the basic government services needed to take advantage of the current recovery?" Trudeau denied the report's findings.

FRANK EDWARDS
The Whig-Standard, Kingston (Ont.), September 30, 1983

CORKY (Violette Clark)
Surrey/North Delta Now, Vancouver, June 17, 1984

AS A RESPECTED ECONOMIST IT IS MY OPINION THAT THE RECESSION WILL RECEDE, INFLATION INFLATE, AND THE ECONOMY ECONOMIZE... UNLESS OF COURSE IT DOESN'T!

MIKE GRASTON
The Windsor Star, March 30, 1984

A dramatic surge of the domestic economic output in January to pre-recession levels led Statistics Canada to report on March 28, 1984, that the recession was now finally over — technically speaking. No doubt the news was little comfort to the unemployed, who comprised almost 12 per cent of the population in 1983. In a report released on September 22, 1983, the Organization for Economic Co-operation and Development, of which Canada is a member, drew attention to Canada for having one of the highest unemployment rates among major industrialized nations.

JOSH BEUTEL
The Telegraph-Journal, Saint John (N.B.), January 9, 1984

DENNIS PRITCHARD
Freelance, Shallow Lake (Ont.), September 23, 1983

CY MORRIS
Union Art Service, Toronto, October 1983

Federal cabinet ministers joined academics, economists and labour leaders in Val-Morin, Quebec, to discuss strategies for combatting unemployment. Employment Minister Lloyd Axworthy revealed some suggestions arising from the meeting. One proposed that the Unemployment Insurance Commission provide funds to create and maintain jobs, not simply to support unemployed people. Another suggestion was that working people should be willing to cooperate with efforts to distribute employment by working and earning less.

Right:
Canadian farm bankruptcies were at their highest level in 1983: 488 were recorded by the Department of Consumer and Corporate Affairs.

LEN NORRIS
The Sun, Vancouver, August 9, 1983

"Well, Dustin, out with it . . . what's this brilliant new concept you're proposing we adopt . . . ?"

EDD ULUSCHAK
The Edmonton Journal, May 16, 1984

DROUGHTS

GRASSHOPPERS

FROSTS

BANKS

Right:

There were no substantial measures included in the $97-billion-dollar budget presented February 15 by Finance Minister Marc Lalonde. This reflected the government's attitude that economic recovery must be spurred mainly by consumers and private businesses rather than by massive amounts of public funding. The budget was criticized for the relatively small increase in job-creation monies it made available despite high unemployment levels. The deficit for the fiscal year beginning April 1, 1984, was projected at $30 billion.

ROI (Roy Carless)
Checkout (United Food and Commercial Workers, Toronto), Fall 1983

"GRAB AHOLD AND WE'LL TAKE YOU IN!"

AISLIN (Terry Mosher)
The Gazette, Montreal, February 16, 1984

JAN KAMIENSKI
The Winnipeg Sun, March 23, 1984

The dollar fell below 80 cents U.S. in February, the first time it had done so in almost two years. Despite massive government support in money markets and rising interest rates, the value of the dollar continued to fall until it crashed through the record low and traded at 75.90 cents U.S. in late June.

VANCE RODEWALT
The Calgary Herald, April 6, 1984

WASHINGTON

ONE DOLLA

DONATO
TORONTO SUN

ANDY DONATO
The Toronto Sun, May 3, 1984

SUE DEWAR
The Calgary Sun, June 1984

ADRIANE RAESIDE
The Times-Colonist, Victoria, June 10, 1984

DUNCAN MACPHERSON
The Toronto Star, May 12, 1984

DUNCAN MACPHERSON
The Toronto Star, May 5, 1984

Canadian interest rates have traditionally been kept marginally higher than those in the United States to attract funds from investors seeking a better return on their capital. But when the Bank of Canada raises its trend-setting interest rates to maintain an edge on U.S. rates, it also discourages consumer spending and corporate investment. Canada's interest-rate policy has been heavily criticized for this reason.

FRANK EDWARDS
The Whig-Standard, Kingston (Ont.), January 20, 1984

The Reagan Administration

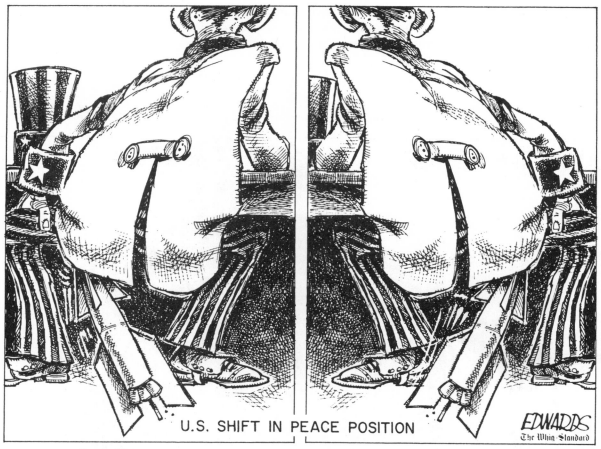

U.S. SHIFT IN PEACE POSITION

FRANK EDWARDS
The Whig-Standard, Kingston (Ont.), May 1984

President Reagan, in a January 16 address on Soviet-U.S. relations, appeared to be departing from his previous hard-line policy by calling for a resumption of nuclear disarmament conferences between the two countries. The Soviet Union had withdrawn from the Geneva conferences in protest against the deployment of U.S. intermediate-range nuclear missiles in Western Europe by members of the North Atlantic Treaty Organization. The only remaining channels of dialogue between the two blocs were the Vienna conferences on conventional force reductions and the thirty-five-nation Stockholm disarmament conference. Political observers speculated that Reagan, wary of the imminent presidential election, was anxious to show progress in Soviet relations and to demonstrate the flexibility of his administration towards disarmament. It was felt, however, that the president offered no substantial proposals on American disarmament. Tass, the official Soviet news agency, was bluntly critical: "Judged by its content, the speech was basically of a propaganda nature."

DALE CUMMINGS
Winnipeg Free Press, January 17, 1984

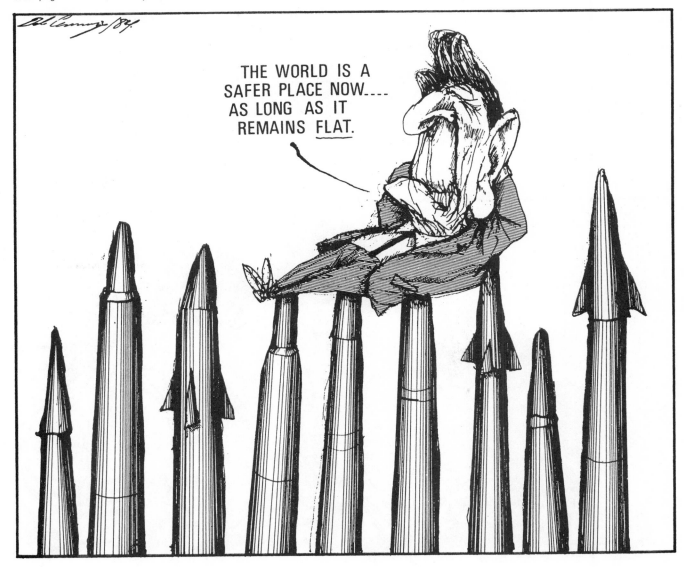

U.S. President Ronald Reagan visited China to strengthen economic, military, and cultural cooperation between the two nations. American recognition of China since the communist revolution has progressed gradually over the years, and American support of Taiwan has been a major obstacle to the improvement of U.S.-Chinese relations. When Chinese leader Deng Xiaoping urged Reagan to promote Taiwan's unification with mainland China, the President replied that the matter had to be worked out between the two countries alone.

Right:

Prime Minister Trudeau met with leaders of six other non-communist nations to discuss and to sign an accord promoting East-West dialogue on peace and disarmament, the central themes of his earlier peace missions. In a heated exchange between Trudeau and Ronald Reagan on relations with the Soviet Union, the president retorted: "Damn it, Pierre . . . what the hell more can I do?" to which Trudeau replied: "For heaven's sake, Ron, do a bit more."

THE TRICK IS TO SNAG THE STEAK WITHOUT DROPPING THE PICKLE

TING (Merle Tingley)
The London Free Press, April 28, 1984

ANDY DONATO
The Toronto Sun, June 12, 1984

The Soviet Union announced on May 7 that it would not attend the Olympic Games in Los Angeles. At least a dozen Soviet-allied countries eventually joined the boycott. Some of the reasons cited for the withdrawal were concern for the safety, rights, and dignity of their athletes. The Soviet government claimed that "chauvinistic and anti-Soviet hysteria are being whipped up" in the United States and that Reagan's administration was "using the games for its own political aims." It was widely speculated that the action was mainly in retaliation for the boycott of the 1980 Olympic Games in Moscow, engineered by then-President Jimmy Carter to protest the Soviet invasion of Afghanistan. About sixty-five countries joined that boycott.

VANCE RODEWALT
The Calgary Herald, May 10, 1984

BADO (Guy Badeaux)
Le Droit, Ottawa, May 12, 1984

The U.S.A.: under Carter . . . under Reagan

Central America and Grenada

On October 25, 1983, 1,900 U.S. Marines and Army Rangers spearheaded an invasion of Grenada, accompanied by police forces of six Caribbean countries, following the assassination of Prime Minister Maurice Bishop of Grenada the week before. The same day, President Reagan announced the invasion to a stunned Congress and public. He defended the intervention by saying it had been urgently requested by the Organization of Eastern Caribbean States "to restore order and democracy" in the wake of the insurrection of the Grenadian government. U.S. Secretary of State George Shultz commented: "We see no responsible government in this country." Grenada was a member of the British Commonwealth and was granted independence in 1974.

ALAN KING
The Citizen, Ottawa, October 29, 1983

DAVID ROSEN
Open City, Montreal, December 1983

President Reagan explained "that a brutal group of leftist thugs violently seized power" on Grenada and that his objectives were to protect the 1,100 U.S. citizens on the island, to evacuate any persons wishing to leave, and to help restore democratic institutions. American forces quickly controlled the island, in the process capturing about 600 Cubans and uncovering caches of Soviet-made small arms and ammunition by the second day. The same day, President Fidel Castro of Cuba announced that there had been 700 Cubans in Grenada, mostly construction workers, including forty military advisers.

ADRIANE RAESIDE
The Times-Colonist, Victoria, November 3, 1983

Opinion of the invasion was widely divergent. The official Soviet news agency, Tass, branded Reagan personally responsible for what it called an "act of undisguised banditry and international terrorism," intended to "subordinate Grenada to U.S. neo-colonialist rule." Members of the Organization of American States also condemned the invasion, declaring it a clear violation of their charter, which bars a state from intervening in the affairs of another member's state. The Organization of Eastern Caribbean States' members that participated in the invasion feared that Grenada's military build-up posed a dangerous threat to the peace and security of other Eastern Caribbean countries. Reagan's administration insisted that the American forces would leave as soon as possible.

BADO (Guy Badeaux)
Le Droit, Ottawa, November 5, 1983

Grenada

MIKE CONSTABLE
Union Art Service, Toronto, November 1983

"*Just erase the bits that mention Vietnam and blip in Central America . . . .*"

On July 26, 1983, only months before the Grenada invasion, President Reagan declared that his administration was not planning a war in nearby Central America and he rejected any comparison between Central America and Vietnam. After the cessation of hostilities in Grenada, the Pentagon reported on November 2 that eighteen U.S. troops had been killed and that ninety-one had been injured.

ADRIANE RAESIDE
The Times-Colonist, Victoria, October 31, 1983

EDD ULUSCHAK
The Edmonton Journal, January 14, 1984

In 1983, President Reagan appointed a national bipartisan commission to make recommendations on U.S. foreign policy regarding Central America. In its report, presented January 11, 1984, the commission recommended an $8-billion-dollar, five-year economic aid program, about double the current level of support. It also recommended increasing military aid to El Salvador. The report gave crucial support to Reagan's own policy towards the region. In his bid to win congressional approval for the aid package, Reagan warned of the Soviet commitment "to change Central America into a string of anti-American, Soviet-styled dictatorships," and he stressed that military force should be "an available part of American foreign policy."

TONY JENKINS
The Globe and Mail, Toronto, April 17, 1984

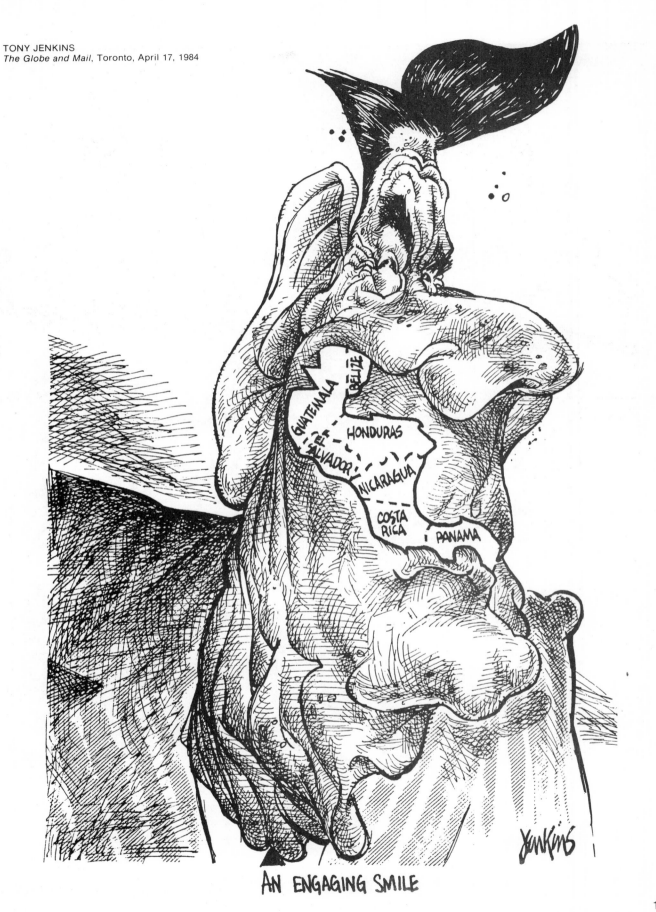

AN ENGAGING SMILE

MIKE GRASTON
The Windsor Star, April 23, 1984

President Reagan appeared on national television on May 9 to appeal for greater public support of his policies towards Central America and to dismiss concerns that his administration had been exaggerating the threat of communist expansion in the region. The president claimed that substantial Soviet aid to Cuba and Nicaragua was designed to foment revolution in the hemisphere. "What we see in El Salvador is an attempt to destabilize the entire region and eventually move chaos and anarchy toward the American border."

KEN MUNRO
Union Art Service, Toronto, June 1984

SUE DEWAR
The Calgary Sun, March 21, 1984

Left:

Attempts to conduct a free presidential election in El Salvador were plagued with bureaucratic difficulties and rebel intimidation designed to disrupt and discredit the election process. After a failed election in March, a run-off between two candidates in May declared the moderate Christian Democrat José Napoleón Duarte to have won narrowly with 53 per cent of the vote. News reports later disclosed that the CIA had committed over $2 million in support of the elections, most of which benefited Duarte and his party.

Below:

Soon after his election, Duarte appealed to the U.S. Congress for more military aid than had been recently made available by President Reagan. Reagan boasted that "Duarte's election was the latest chapter in a trend toward democracy throughout Latin America."

EDD ULUSCHAK
The Edmonton Journal, May 28, 1984

On August 8, the Guatemalan military overthrew the regime of José Efrain Ríos Montt, a born-again Christian who was a member of Church of the Word, a fundamentalist Protestant sect based in California. Montt had assumed power following a military coup in 1982 and his administration was accused by the army of religious fanaticism that "violated the fundamental principle of separation of Church and State." The army command immediately lifted restrictions on civil liberties imposed by Montt and also pledged to end the secret trials of suspected terrorists which had resulted in the execution of fifteen people. General Oscar Mejia promised a return to the democratic process by first legalizing political parties and then holding elections within one year for a representative assembly. He would turn over power only to an elected president.

DAVE CUMMINGS
Winnipeg Free Press, August 10, 1983

THE FACE OF GUATEMALAN DEMOCRACY

The Middle East and Africa

GAMBOLI (Tony Harpes)
The Gazette, Montreal, June 1984

BOB KRIEGER
The Province, Vancouver, October 25, 1983

About 240 U.S. Marines and sailors, members of a multinational peacekeeping force in Lebanon, died in a suicide terrorist attack on the Marine headquarters near Beirut on October 23, 1983. A truck laden with TNT crashed through the defences of the compound at dawn and was driven into the barracks where it was detonated by the driver. Moments later, in a virtually identical attack on the nearby French barracks, almost sixty French paratroopers were killed. Circumstantial evidence at the time pointed to Iranian and perhaps Syrian complicity in the killings, according to U.S. officials.

EDD ULUSCHAK
The Edmonton Journal, October 25, 1983

Digging in

ADRIANE RAESIDE
The Times-Colonist, Victoria, November 20, 1983

Left:
Yasir Arafat, chairman of the Palestinian Liberation Organization, and his loyalists were gradually surrounded and overrun in Tripoli, Lebanon, by Palestinian rebels backed by Syria. Tripoli had been on the verge of destruction as the rebels threatened to eradicate Arafat's forces if they did not leave the city. Arafat vowed to "continue to fight to the end." Both sides accepted a Saudi Arabian cease-fire plan that called for the evacuation of all armed combatants, the unity of the PLO, and the settling of differences by political means. About 500 people had been killed and over 1,500 wounded in two weeks of fighting.

Below:
A crippling international trade deficit and drastic currency devaluation spurred inflation in Israel to 190 per cent during 1983. The country's 350,000-member civil service protested the erosion of their wages by engaging in strikes and slowdowns for almost two months.

MIKE CONSTABLE
Union Art Service, Toronto, January 1984

A steadily worsening state of civil war in Beirut, aggravated by Syrian aggression on Lebanon, prompted President Reagan on February 7 to withdraw the U.S. Marines who had been stationed there as part of the multinational peacekeeping force. Other countries promptly followed suit. Only days before, Lebanese President Amin Gemayel had pleaded with the U.S. Congress to maintain its support of the peacekeeping force. He warned that if the U.S. Marines were to be withdrawn, his government would be replaced by "a revolutionary council under Soviet control, or chaos."

LEBANESE FLAG
new design

DALE CUMMINGS
Winnipeg Free Press, September 20, 1983

BOB KRIEGER
The Province, Vancouver, February 9, 1984

TONY JENKINS
The Globe and Mail, Toronto, May 22, 1984

Hostilities in the three-and-a-half-year-long war between Iran and Iraq escalated dramatically in 1984 and culminated in a rash of air attacks by the two countries on foreign-owned ships in the northern Persian Gulf. In February, both countries began bombarding civilian centres for the first time. Iraq then blockaded Kharg Island, Iran's main oil export terminal, to press Iran into negotiating an end to hostilities. Iran retaliated by striking at foreign ships en route to or from Iraq; Iraq replied in kind.

ALAN KING
The Citizen, Ottawa, May 19, 1984

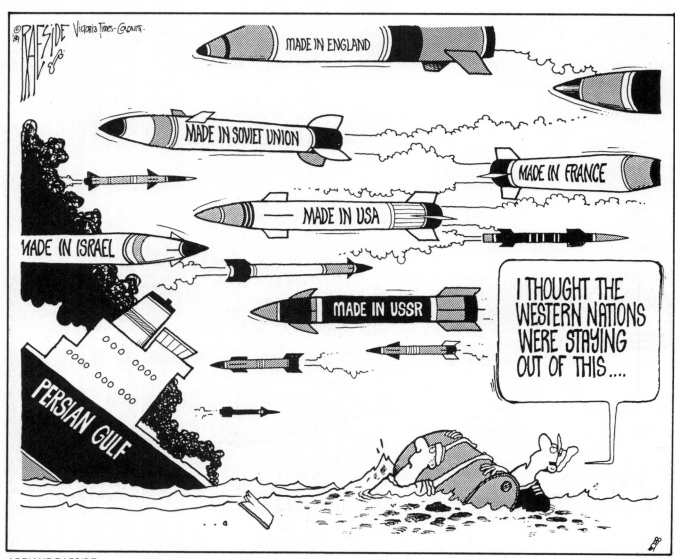

ADRIANE RAESIDE
The Times-Colonist, Victoria, May 27, 1984

Left:
The air attacks on foreign ships in the Persian Gulf touched off a wave of panic among shipping and ship insurance companies. Predictably, though, the war planes and armaments used in the war were supplied by those countries that were anxious to maintain stability in the Persian Gulf.

Below:
It was learned that about 240 Iranian prisoners of war held by Iraq were between the ages of twelve and eighteen. A United Nations commission on human rights condemned the practice and called on Iran to stop recruiting children. Iran claimed that the recruitment was not an established practice.

JAN KAMIENSKI
The Winnipeg Sun, March 13, 1984

The Gulf War

Below:

A diplomatic crisis erupted in April 1984, following a shooting incident at the Libyan embassy in London, England. A group of exiled Libyan demonstrators, protesting the regime of Colonel Muammar Khadafy, were attacked by machine-gun fire from within the embassy building. Ten demonstrators were injured and a British policewoman was killed. British attempts to seek out the gunmen were unsuccessful and the two countries promptly ended diplomatic relations.

Right:

The escalation of Libyan air attacks on Chad, in August 1983, inflicted heavy civilian casualties and fuelled speculation that Chadian President Hissene Habre had been killed. Chad's foreign ministry denied Libyan news reports to that effect, saying, "It's not the first time the Libyans have announced that we are all dead."

DALE CUMMINGS
Winnipeg Free Press, April 19, 1984

"The first three rows are for each time I killed the president of Chad . . ."

ROY PETERSON
The Sun, Vancouver, August 4, 1983

Korean Air Lines Flight 007

A Korean Air Lines jumbo jet, which strayed into restricted Soviet air space over Sakhalin Island in the Sea of Japan, was shot down by a Soviet fighter plane on September 1, 1983, killing all 269 occupants aboard, including ten Canadians. Shock and anger concerning the incident were expressed around the world as many countries assailed the Soviet Union for attacking a defenceless civilian aircraft. In its official explanation of the incident, the Soviet administration charged that the United States had engineered the plane's flight over sensitive military installations as part of a surveillance mission carried out by an American spy plane that was also in the vicinity of the incident. They further charged that the plane had ignored recognized warning signals and had attempted to resist detection by flying without its navigation lights.

ALAN KING
The Citizen, Ottawa, September 3, 1983

BOB KRIEGER
The Province, Vancouver, September 12, 1983

BADO (Guy Badeaux)
Le Droit, Ottawa, September 30, 1983

"What South Korean plane? I didn't see anything in the paper."

The Canadian government suspended for sixty days Canadian landing rights for Aeroflot, the official Soviet airline, in a punitive gesture to the country. It further claimed $2.1 million in damages on behalf of the families of the Canadians killed in the accident. The Soviet embassy immediately refused the demand and declared the U.S. government responsible for allegedly directing the South Korean plane.

ROY PETERSON
The Sun, Vancouver, September 7, 1983

"In Canada we can be quite rough on mass murderers, Mr. Andropov — 60 days loss of privileges!"

Prime Minister Trudeau tried to downplay censure of the Soviet leadership for the incident and instead blamed the Soviet fighter pilot and his commander for what he called "a tragic accident." Opposition leader Brian Mulroney took a harder line towards the Soviet government and criticized Trudeau for not treating the incident as an act of murder. Mulroney's views appeared to echo those of President Reagan who warned, "We live in a dangerous world with cruel people . . . who disregard individual rights and the value of human life." Despite Reagan's tone, his administration did not enact any major retaliatory measures against the Soviet Union.

DUNCAN MACPHERSON
The Toronto Star, October 8, 1983

ANDY DONATO
The Toronto Sun, October 6, 1983

Disarmament

Below:
"The World After Nuclear War" was the theme of a conference of scientists from the United States, the Soviet Union, and other countries who met in Washington, D.C., to discuss their research on the possible long-term effects of nuclear war. One of the group's most significant findings was a warning that even a limited nuclear exchange could so alter the earth's climate that the northern hemisphere would suffer months of cold and darkness.

Right:
June 6, 1984, marked the fortieth anniversary of D-Day, the Allied landing on the beaches of Normandy in Nazi-occupied France during the Second World War. Canada provided one-fifth of the assault forces in the critical invasion, which liberated France and led the way to Allied victory.

DENNIS PRITCHARD
Freelance, Shallow Lake (Ont.), November 18, 1983

156

AISLIN (Terry Mosher)
The Gazette, Montreal, June 6, 1984

"Good luck, buddy . . ." *"You too, pal."*

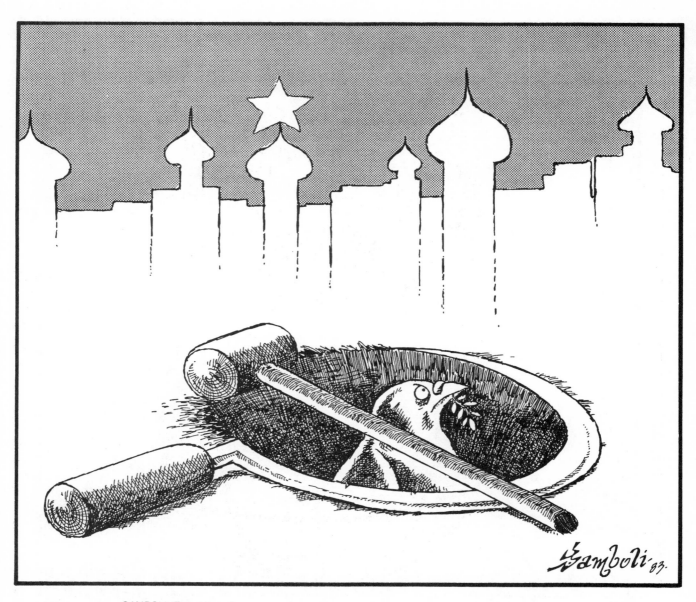

GAMBOLI (Tony Harpes)
The Gazette, Montreal, December 3, 1983

Soviet retaliation to the announced deployment of 572 U.S. intermediate-range missiles in Western Europe by the North Atlantic Treaty Organization was swift and unequivocal. President Yuri Andropov announced on November 23 that his country would withdraw from the Geneva conferences on nuclear weapons reductions. Other countermeasures included an increase in the number of submarines off the U.S. coast carrying nuclear missiles reportedly capable of striking U.S. targets within ten minutes.

DENNIS PRITCHARD
Freelance, Shallow Lake (Ont.), May 24, 1984

Right:
Peace groups protesting the controversial planned testing of unarmed cruise missiles in Canada were dealt a harsh reply by Prime Minister Trudeau. He said his government would remain faithful in its commitments to allies in the North Atlantic Treaty Organizations as long as Canada continued to be a member of NATO.

SID BARRON
The Toronto Star, February 5, 1984

". . . third world war souvenirs . . . get them now before it's too late . . . souvenirs . . ."

VANCE RODEWALT
The Calgary Sun, July 27, 1983

THE SCRUISE MISSILE

The Environment

It is estimated that American pollution is responsible for at least half the acid rain falling on Canada. Canada's efforts to protect its environment are frustrated by this fact, since effective control requires the cooperation of both countries. After the U.S. administration decided on January 25 to postpone pollution control measures pending more research, the Canadian government reacted angrily. The statement issued by the Canadian embassy in Washington declared, "The continued delay in adopting effective abatement measures is not acceptable to Canada."

ALAN KING
The Citizen, Ottawa, March 23, 1984

THOSE CANADIANS ARE ALWAYS YAPPING ABOUT ACID RAIN. LOOKS TO ME LIKE THOSE FISH ARE VICTIMS OF SUN-STROKE

MIKE CONSTABLE
Union Art Service, Toronto, March 1984

ALAN KING
The Citizen, Ottawa, February 21, 1984

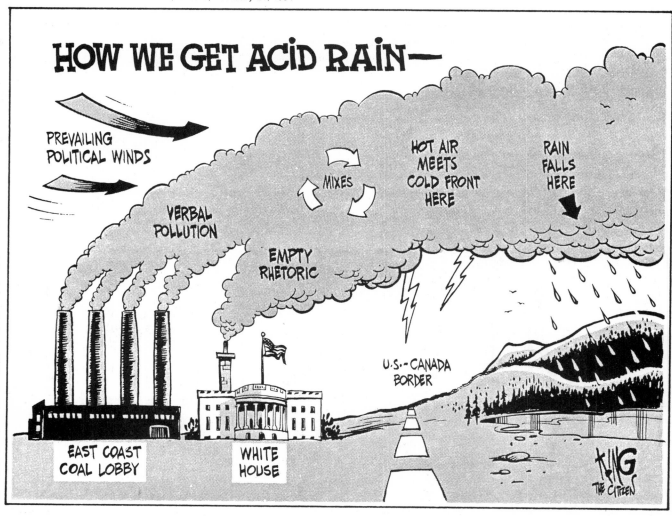

Security and Defence

Canada's armed forces operated with a budget of almost $8 million during 1983-84. However, critics have long doubted the ability of the force to fulfil its foremost mandate, to protect Canada's sovereignty.

BOB BIERMAN
Freelance, Victoria, September 1983

Right:
The sixteen member countries of the North Atlantic Treaty Organization met in Washington to affirm their commitment to a military arms build-up. At the same time, they expressed their interest in negotiating with the Soviet Union mutual curbs on arms proliferation, both nuclear and conventional.

JAN KAMIENSKI
The Winnipeg Sun, May 27, 1984

JOHN LARTER
The Toronto Star, May 23, 1984

TING (Merle Tingley)
The London Free Press, March 7, 1984

Testing of an air-launched, unarmed cruise missile began on March 6, promptly after a Federal Court of Appeal dismissed a request by anti-nuclear groups to grant an injunction against the testing.

Provincial Affairs

The province of Alberta conducted a two-and-a-half-month-long education program in 1983 to combat racism. Concern developed especially after Jim Keegstra, a former high-school teacher and mayor of Eckville, received nationwide attention for reportedly propagating racial hatred and for telling his pupils that the Holocaust was a hoax.

ALAN KING
The Citizen, Ottawa, October 19, 1983

Below:
Alberta's treasury announced an increase of about 13 per cent in the province's personal income tax rate to reduce the large budgetary deficit. Despite the fact that the Heritage Savings Trust Fund was endowed with $13 billion generated from petroleum royalties and investments, Premier Peter Lougheed insisted that the fund was to be regarded as a "rainy days" savings account, to be used when oil revenues eventually declined.

Right:
The proposed Canada Health Act pitted Federal Health Minister Monique Begin against Alberta's Hospitals Minister Dave Russell over the issue of providing medicare services to citizens whose premiums had fallen into arrears. The act would insist on full patient coverage at all times, and would allow the federal government to withhold transfer payments, on a dollar for dollar basis, to provinces that charged hospital user fees or that permitted extra billing by doctors.

ROI (Roy Carless)
Impact (Alberta Union of Public Employees), Winter 1983

"SORRY! IT ONLY OPENS WHEN WE DIAL E-L-E-C-T-I-O-N!"

VANCE RODEWALT
The Calgary Herald, February 22, 1984

The issue of increasing constitutional protection of French-language rights and of guaranteeing limited bilingual government services in Manitoba was hotly debated following the NDP government's attempts to introduce legislation benefiting the province's 60,000 francophones. Public hearings and plebiscites on the subject indicated that the majority of Manitobans rejected the language package, and obstructive tactics by the Tory opposition jammed Premier Howard Pawley's attempts to pass the legislation. A challenge of Manitoba's English-only statutes was before the Supreme Court of Canada at the time, and an all-party resolution of the House of Commons backed the proposed legislation.

ANTHONY DELATRI
Le Nouvelliste, Trois-Rivières (Que.), February 14, 1984

Manitoba: the two languages

BOB KRIEGER
The Province, Vancouver, February 26, 1984

BICKERSTAFF (Don Evans)
The Orillia Sun (Ont.), November 30, 1983

Left:
A resolution advanced in the Ontario Legislature by the New Democratic Party to declare Ontario a nuclear-free zone was soundly defeated on November 25 by the government of Premier Bill Davis. The motion was intended to prohibit all activities related to nuclear armaments or their components, including manufacture, transportation, and testing.

Below:
The third session of Ontario's thirty-second Parliament, which ended on December 16, was observed to be one of the quietest sessions in recent history. Two of the more significant bills introduced during 1983 were ones adopting French as an official language of the province's courts and another granting all Ontario francophones the right to an education in French.

AISLIN (Terry Mosher)
The Gazette, Montreal, December 19, 1983

175

Below:

One proposal put forth to deal with the problem of street soliciting by prostitutes in Vancouver was to issue them licences and permit them to solicit privately in a designated area of the city. Citizens' groups and civic officials anxious to curtail the street activity had met with little success since police must prove that soliciting has been "pressing or persistent."

Right:

The British Columbia government enacted changes to the province's labour code in an attempt to reduce the number of large-scale strikes that aggravated the province's poor economy. The amendment imposed greater restrictions on strike action and provided union members more freedom to dissent.

LEN NORRIS
The Sun, Vancouver, January 14, 1984

". . . but my wife is bound to ask me what my new position is . . ."

...AND FROM THE SOCIETY THAT BROUGHT YOU THE DISPOSABLE DIAPER... THE DISPOSABLE RAZOR AND THE DISPOSABLE LIGHTER... WE'RE EXTREMELY PROUD TO INTRODUCE THE NEW...1984...

DISPOSABLE WORKER!

KEN MUNRO
Union Art Service, Toronto, June 1984

Quebec

"The aspirations of our society are linked with the accession of Quebec to sovereignty." So read part of a policy statement prepared by the executives of the Parti Québécois, Quebec's governing separatist party, that recommended the principles of the party's next election platform. The party's commitment to independence worried many party members at a time when popular support for Premier René Lévesque and his party had fallen to very low levels. A poll by Centre de researche sur l'opinion publique released on January 18 indicated that 66 per cent of decided voters would support the provincial Liberal party in an election, versus only 24 per cent for the Parti Québécois.

ANTHONY DELATRI
Le Nouvelliste, Trois-Rivières (Que.), February 16, 1984

Patience! Patience! The wind will change!

TONY JENKINS
The Globe and Mail, Toronto, June 12, 1984

MONSIEUR LEVESQUE WALKS HIS LEMMINGS

Left:
Members of the Parti Québécois met for a biennial convention in Montreal on June 8 to thrash out the party's platform for the upcoming election. Delegates voted overwhelmingly to adopt a resolution declaring Quebec sovereignty as the central ideology of the party. This hard-line stance contrasted with René Lévesque's earlier attempts to soft-pedal independence under the name of "sovereignty-association."

ANTHONY DELATRI
Le Nouvelliste, Trois-Rivières (Que.), December 16, 1983

Next Election: Independence

ANTHONY DELATRI
Le Nouvelliste, Trois-Rivières (Que.), December 28, 1983

Exchange Counter . . . Public opinion poll

ROY PETERSON
The Sun, Vancouver, October 7, 1983

A poll conducted by *Le Devoir*, Radio Canada, and English radio station CJAD produced somewhat confusing results. It found that a majority of Quebeckers felt Pierre Trudeau would be most likely to defeat the Progressive Conservative party of Brian Mulroney. It also found that most respondents believed Trudeau and René Lévesque should both resign as leaders of their respective parties.

Below:

The Quebec government announced that it would open an office in Ottawa to monitor federal programs and legislative developments affecting the province. The office, similar to ones in Edmonton, Toronto, and Moncton, would cost almost half a million dollars per year to operate.

Right:

Premier René Lévesque announced his government's largest shuffle of cabinet ministers in an apparent attempt to improve the much-beleaguered image of his administration. The move, which Quebec Liberal leader Robert Bourassa likened to "a game of musical chairs," mainly transferred responsibilities among some top-ranking ministers but also introduced the first anglophone to the separatist government.

ANTHONY DELATRI
Le Nouvelliste, Trois-Rivières (Que.), May 7, 1984

Official delegation to Ottawa . . . Republic of Quebec

AISLIN (Terry Mosher)
The Gazette, Montreal, March 7, 1984

186

SUE DEWAR
The Calgary Sun, April 15, 1984

Left:
Liberal leadership candidate John Turner found himself inadvertently playing into the hands of René Lévesque when Turner remarked that language rights are a provincial matter, in reference to Manitoba's controversial French-language-rights debate. Quebec's Charter of the French Language, popularly known as Bill 101, designates French as the only official language of the province and places substantial restrictions on the use of other languages.

Below:
Former Quebec Premier Robert Bourassa was overwhelmingly re-elected leader of the provincial Liberal party on October 15 after absenting himself from politics since 1976. Bourassa served two terms as premier, from 1970 to 1976, but promptly resigned as leader of his party following its crushing defeat to the Parti Québécois.

DAVID ROSEN
Open City, Montreal, December 1983

AISLIN (Terry Mosher)
The Gazette, Montreal, April 6, 1984

Lotteries

News of a growing, unclaimed jackpot in the weekly 6/49 lottery spurred wild ticket sales until a prize of almost $14 million went to a working couple in Brantford, Ontario. The win was the largest tax-free prize in North American history.

ANTHONY DELATRI
Le Nouvelliste, Trois-Rivières (Que.), January 5, 1984

In Pakistan . . . In Quebec this week . . .

JAN KAMIENSKI
The Winnipeg Sun, March 15, 1984

The federal government's decision to launch a weekly baseball betting pool, called Sport Select Baseball, was challenged by nine of the ten provinces on the grounds that it violated a 1979 agreement giving provinces the exclusive right to operate lotteries. The federal government contended that such a pool was not limited by the agreement because, unlike lotteries, the game involved some measure of skill. The pool was designed to provide funds for amateur athletic competition.

VANCE RODEWALT
The Calgary Herald, May 2, 1984

BILL SCHAEFER
The Waterloo Chronicle (Ont.), May 9, 1984

Shortly after the launch of Sport Select Baseball on May 1, 1984, the Canadian Sports Pool Corporation lost thousands of ticket retailers, mainly on account of strong pressure from the provincial lottery corporations.

LEN NORRIS
The Sun, Vancouver, June 5, 1984

"Mind you, we had hoped Roger's reward for faithful party service would be a less-controversial appointment to the Senate . . ."

Social Attitudes

SID BARRON
The Toronto Star, August 1983

"... hey, I just felt a slight twinge of pride in being Canadian ... second time this year ... not as strong as that one back in February ... that was a really big one ..."

Major amendments to Canada's Divorce Act were introduced in the Commons that would greatly simplify and reduce the cost and length of divorce proceedings. Among these, simple marriage breakdown would be sufficient grounds for divorce; no longer would the fault of one spouse be required, as it must be for the current grounds of adultery, desertion, and mental or physical cruelty. The trial period for obtaining divorce would be reduced to only one year and uncontested applications could be handled out of court. It was estimated that legal costs could be reduced by as much as one-half by the proposed amendments.

BLAINE
The Hamilton Spectator, March 13, 1984

"ABSOLUTELY NO MORE CANADIAN FISH FOR US, MAJOR, UNTIL THIS BEASTLINESS TOWARD THE BABY SEALS IS ENDED."

CY MORRIS
Union Art Service, Toronto, May 1984

Left:
The International Fund for Animal Welfare had been promoting a boycott in the United States and Great Britain of Canadian fish products, to pressure the Canadian government to ban the much-publicized baby seal hunt. The attempts of the IFAW to monitor the hunt by helicopter in March were thwarted when angry residents of the Magdalen Islands smashed and overturned their craft.

SID BARRON
The Toronto Star, September 18, 1983

" . . . that you, Martha? Hey, I've just been looking through your new Vogue . . . they've really gone too far this time . . . nobody will ever wear this stuff. . . ."

SID BARRON
The Toronto Star, May 13, 1984

"... way deep down I think what would make me deliriously optimistic
about Canada is, like if we could somehow clean out all the politicians
and the entire civil service we are blessed with today and start all over
again ..."

BOB BIERMAN
Freelance, Victoria, date unavailable

Miscellany

Below:

An Air Canada Boeing 767 jet ran out of fuel and was forced to make an emergency landing on July 23 at an abandoned airstrip in Manitoba, while en route to Edmonton from Ottawa. Because of a failure of the plane's fuel gauge system, the plane's fuel volume was measured manually before take-off, but was converted to fuel weight incorrectly. The airline blamed human error for the faulty conversion from Imperial to metric measure.

Right:

A dispute among European Community members arose over Great Britain's claim that it was making overpayments to the ECs fund. Prime Minister Margaret Thatcher had demanded rebates and smaller payments for Britain because the country's benefits from the fund, mainly in the form of agricultural subsidies, were far outstripped by the country's contributions to the fund. Thatcher's administration considered withholding Britain's regular EC payments to press for reforms to the policy but this move ultimately was not necessary.

ADRIANE RAESIDE
The Times-Colonist, Victoria, August 3, 1983

SUSAN DEWAR
The Calgary Sun, March 23, 1984

JIM TODD
Cameron Publications, N.S., January 13, 1984

Left:

In April 1984, Donald Marshall, a Micmac Indian who had served eleven years of a life sentence for murder, was awarded $25,000 in interim compensation by the Nova Scotia government after he was cleared of the crime in 1983. Attorney General Ronald Giffin had been under mounting public pressure to provide compensation for Marshall and also to repay his estimated $87,000 in legal costs.

Below:

The Canada Health Act, approved by all parties of Parliament on April 9, was intended to improve access to medical care by preventing the provinces from permitting extra billing by doctors and hospital user fees, for those services provided under provincial medicare programs. Beginning July 1, the federal government would be entitled to withhold transfer payments to a province in the amount of the illegally charged fees.

CY MORRIS
Union Art Service, Toronto, February 1984

Below:

A twelve-minute film entitled *Excuse Me, But There's a Computer Asking For You*, prepared for Revenue Canada, was intended to make taxpayers wary of cheating on their income tax returns. The film depicts an all-knowing computer programmed to investigate, cross reference, and identify offenders. It was first shown on CBC on January 30 and was quickly scorned by Tory MPs as being oppressive and fearsome.

Right:

Extensive renovations of the Statue of Liberty, famous symbol of America's freedom, began in January at a cost of $210 million (U.S.). Funds provided entirely by private donations will employ about sixty craftsmen and machinists to complete the repairs that will take over two years.

GAMBOLI (Tony Harpes)
The Gazette, Montreal, February 25, 1984

BADO (Guy Badeaux)
Le Droit, Ottawa, April 24, 1984

Past Award Winners

The National Newspaper Award — Editorial Cartoon

1949	Jack Boothe, *The Globe and Mail*, Toronto
1950	James G. Reidford, *The Montreal Star*
1951	Leonard Norris, *The Vancouver Sun*
1952	Robert La Palme, *Le Devoir*, Montreal
1953	Robert W. Chambers, *The Chronicle-Herald*, Halifax
1954	John Collins, *The Gazette*, Montreal
1955	Merle R. Tingley, *The London Free Press*
1956	James G. Reidford, *The Globe and Mail*, Toronto
1957	James G. Reidford, *The Globe and Mail*, Toronto
1958	Raoul Hunter, *Le Soleil*, Quebec City
1959	Duncan Macpherson, *The Toronto Star*
1960	Duncan Macpherson, *The Toronto Star*
1961	Ed McNally, *The Montreal Star*
1962	Duncan Macpherson, *The Toronto Star*
1963	Jan Kamienski, *The Winnipeg Tribune*
1964	Ed McNally, *The Montreal Star*
1965	Duncan Macpherson, *The Toronto Star*
1966	Robert W. Chambers, *The Chronicle-Herald*, Halifax
1967	Raoul Hunter, *Le Soleil*, Quebec City
1968	Roy Peterson, *The Vancouver Sun*
1969	Edd Uluschak, *The Edmonton Journal*
1970	Duncan Macpherson, *The Toronto Star*
1971	Yardley Jones, *The Toronto Sun*
1972	Duncan Macpherson, *The Toronto Star*
1973	John Collins, *The Gazette*, Montreal
1974	Blaine, *The Hamilton Spectator*
1975	Roy Peterson, *The Vancouver Sun*
1976	Andy Donato, *The Toronto Sun*
1977	Terry Mosher (Aislin), *The Gazette*, Montreal
1978	Terry Mosher (Aislin), *The Gazette*, Montreal
1979	Edd Uluschak, *The Edmonton Journal*
1980	Victor Roschkov, *The Toronto Star*
1981	Tom Innes, *The Calgary Herald*
1982	Blaine, *The Hamilton Spectator*

Index

MIKE GRASTON
The Windsor Star, March 1, 1984